A RAINBOW BABY

A Rainbow of Hope After the Storm

WRITTEN BY
CRYSTAL FALK

A Rainbow Baby Book

What is a Rainbow Baby?

A rainbow baby is a baby who is born after a parent has experienced a miscarriage, stillbirth or infant loss.

The thought is, the loss is like a storm and the baby who follows is like the rainbow. After a storm, a rainbow filled with hope may appear. Although there are still dark clouds above, there is hope and joy that follows the storm.

NOTE: Most mental health care experts believe that death should be explained briefly but honestly to young children. The words chosen fall in line with that thinking.

Add your special angel(s) here:

_____

Add your special rainbow(s) here:

_____

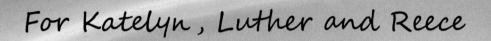

For Katelyn, Luther and Reece

Angel Babies

Addison Wolf	Baby Cardona	Boo
AJ Gorton	Baby Davis	Braidyn Wayne
Alessia Theresa Gale	Baby Flores	Brandon
Alexis Nicole Crane	Baby Hadley	Brantley James Adams
Alyssa Kathleen Schmalzriedt	Baby John	Carmello Michael
Anaiah Elizabeth Tarrats	Baby Mena 1	Castillo Angels
Angel Agron	Baby Mena 2	Charlie
Angel Gale	Baby Mena 3	Charlotte Bethany Hegarty-Lovejoy
Angel Gale	Baby Ramsey	Chloe
Angel Gale	Baby Rohman	Chloe Lorelei
Angel Gale	Baby Ruiz	Creed Gabriel
Angel Gale	Baby Saric	Cristian Andres Laluz
Angel Gale	Baby Scott	Daniel Pate
Angel Wolf	Baby Sivertsen	Devin Oliver
Angel-Lia Juline Dauzart	Baby Trotter	Dwayne Oliver
Aranda Babies	Baby Waters	Emma Kate
Averi Wolf	Baby Wentzek	Fowler Angels
Baby Alvizo	Baby Wentzek	Gabriel
Baby Boy Ramsey	Blueberry	Gabriel Lee

"All children are miracles, even the ones that couldn't stay very long."

Rainbow Babies

Addison Dawn	Edwin Johan	Jeff Pratt
Addison Grace	Eli James	Jensen Trace Scott
Adler Joel	Eliana Hope Mena	Jessalyn Diane
Alfie Benjamin Paul Lovejoy	Elijah Jeremiah Mena	Jonathan Adrian Laluz
Amelia Mae Fowler	Eliza rose-ann	Jordan Robert
Andrew Pate Jr	Elliana Isabel	Josiah
Anthony Tom Oliver	Emersyn Mae	Judon Rain Dauzart
Arabella Dawn	Faith Morgan Gouge	Julianna Hope
Baby Wolf	Gabriel London	Kaida Lee
Bentley Everardo Ruiz	Gannon Jace	Kayden Jaques
Bow Pedwell	Gianna Lei	Kaylani Ruby
Caleb Monroe	Gilbert Rainwater	Kaylea Ann Schmalzriedt
Chance Wentzek	Giovanni Vincent	Kendall Elizabeth
Charlotte Elizabeth Marie	Hailey	Khaleesi Izabel
Courtney	Iker Flores	Knox Hurley
Damian Jude	Jacob Andrew	Kyle
Dixon Liam	Jade Rose Lee Aranda	Kyle Current
Dominick Dylan	Jarod Current	Kynley Belle
Donovan Phoenix	Jasmine Nevaeh	Liam Cameron Gollaba

"There is a Rainbow of Hope After Every Storm"

Angel Babies

George	Melissa Kathleen Pratt	The Three Hurley Angels
Grace Shannon Gouge	Michael	Tim Mear
Gracelyn Marie	Nathaniel Holliday	Tina White
Gunner Brian	Payton Rey	Toby Magrath
Harper Wolf	Phoenix Hope	Todd Moore
Harrison-ryan	Prezlynn McLeary	Tony Pedwell
Hartleigh Ray	Quincy Oliver	Tony Watt
Iris Frances Johnson	Ramon Pedwell	Travis John
Isabella Faith Mena	Raymond III	Trisha Branch
Isaiah Hoyt	Reagan Elizabeth	Tyler Red
Jaycob Ryan	Reagan Stanley	Vance Davis
Jewelianna	Rebekah Marjorie Current	Vincent Jones
Joseph Matthew Pierce	River Skye	Walter Anderson
Kasai' Amir Franklin	Ronald Kenneth Leo Johnson	Warren Miller
Kattie Kay	Rose Lynn	Wayne Taylor
Khloe Grace	Seraphina Indigo	Westly Moore
Leilani Giselle	Sydney Elle Gollaba	Willow Irene
Macey	Sydney Mae	Yasmine Davis
Mason	Temperance Mae	Emilia Morgan Claytor

"All children are miracles, even the
ones that couldn't stay very long."

Rainbow Babies

Lillian Magrath	Sally Plain	Tate Hurley
Lily Rae Johnson	Samson Luke	Taylor Queen
Linnea Rae Leigh Pierce	Sawyer Elijah	Taylor Young
Lydia Lynn Schmalzriedt	Scarlet Gorton	Thomas White
Macey	Scarlett	Thompson Joe
Madison Rose	Scott Roman	Timothy T
Mathew Magrath	Sean Johnson	Tom Smith
Matias Saric	Seanna Grace	Tony Smith
Michaela Rosa	Shawn Brown	Wade True
Neela Sivertsen	Skie White	Wednesday Oillie
Nevaeh	Skipper Lay	West Johnson
Nicholas Orion	Sky Green	West Reid
Phoebe Hurley	Skylar Jackson	William Asher
Preston Mcleary	Sofia Julia Gale	William Hue
Quinn Alora	Sofie Ryan	William S
Raylyn Grace	Sunny Johnson	Willson Valintine
Rayne Florence	Susan Little	Willy Silver
Richard Joseph Mena III	Suzie Robert	Danielle Morgan Claytor
Rosalie Renee	Tammy Lee	Charleigh Johanne Claytor

"There is a Rainbow of Hope After Every Storm"

"Mom, Dad! Lets go! Lets go!" Anna exclaimed impatiently. The little girl stood at the front door with her shoes on and her backpack filled with items for a beautiful family day at the beach.

Anna loved to play outside and spend time with her mother and father. She also loved to go to the beach and feel the sand between her toes. Today Anna and her parents were planning to spend a day at the beach just as they did every year.

After some time, Anna's parents were ready to leave. Her father held a collapsed beach umbrella while her mom carried the family beach bag. Anna and her parents were ready and excited for their day at the beach.

As Anna opened the door, her huge smile and joy quickly faded. The once sunny day filled with white fluffy clouds had been replaced by dark gray rain clouds. "Oh dear, it looks like it is going to rain," Anna's mother said sadly.

"Can we still go to the beach Momma?" Anna asked. "Sadly, we will have to wait to see if the weather clears up. If it doesn't, we will reschedule our day to the beach."

Anna was sad. She walked back into the house and sat in the living room near the window and watched as more and more dark clouds filled the once sunny sky. Then it began to rain. First slow and then fast and hard.

Everything that was once dry was now wet. The sidewalk, Anna's swing and outdoor toys. "Momma, I didn't think it was going to rain" she said in a very sad tone. "Me neither," Anna's mom answered.

Suddenly lightning struck and thunder roared. "Boom!" the thunder let out.
"Mommy!" Anna screamed as she hopped up and ran into her mother's arms.
"There, there Anna," her mother said as she wrapped her arms around Anna.

"Although storms can be very scary, they can also bring something beautiful. Do you know what that is Anna?" Anna's mother said. "What's that Momma?" Anna asked. "They can bring beautiful rainbows."

"One day before you were born, we were expecting another baby. Your father and I were very excited to meet him. Day by day, we waited as he grew bigger and stronger. One day, he stopped growing. His body stopped working and sadly, he died."

Mommy and Daddy felt scared and very sad when your brother died. It was like a storm had come. The storm left us very sad and scared. We didn't know when or if the rain would stop. It was a very sad time in our lives.

Days, weeks and months went by. Every day we hoped to see the rain clear and the skies become sunny again. One day, the rain slowed down. Just like the rain, the sadness was still there but something amazing was about to happen. We found out we were going to have you Anna, our beautiful rainbow baby. A beautiful rainbow that came after our storm.

"Even though our beautiful rainbow appeared after our storm, we will never forget the storm that came before. Sometimes other families go through storms just like we did. Some experience the joy of having a rainbow after a storm while others do not." "So I am a rainbow?" Anna asked. "Yes Sweetie, you are our rainbow." Anna's Dad explained. He then pulled out a picture that was taken after she was born.

"Mommy, Daddy, I have one more question" Anna asked quietly. "Yes Anna" they responded. "Since rainbows are found outside, can I go outside now? I really want to go to the beach and it looks like the rain has stopped." Anna's parents smiled and let out a laugh. "I guess rainbows should be outside."

Anna was right. The rain had stopped and the sun came out from behind the clouds. The storm ended shortly after it had begun. Anna, her mother and father all packed up and went to the beach. As they were walking up to Anna's favorite spot on the beach, a beautiful rainbow stretched across the sky showing it's bright, beautiful colors.

Anna was so excited to see the rainbow. Anna and her parents built sandcastles, collected seashells and spent the rest of the day together as the rainbow shined down on them. Although Anna was never able to meet her big brother and play with him on the beach, Anna and her parents remembered him everywhere they went. Their love for him was never-ending. And that's the story of the rainbow of hope after the storm.

About the Author

Crystal Falk has been writing children's books on sensitive subjects since she became a surrogate mother in 2013. Her educational background in art, graphic design and creative writing as well as her experience with sensitive topics gives her a unique perspective which she incorporates into her writing.

When Crystal is not writing children's books, she is spending time with her three children, husband and dog.

Crystal has authored several books along with her co-author Kim Roman. Books include A Rainbow Baby Story, Sophia's Broken Crayons, Dino Hero as well as Grown in Another Garden.

Made in the USA
Middletown, DE
23 October 2020